Prisoners In The North

The Forgotten Deaths at Harperley Camp

John Ruttley.

ISBN No 0-9543360-1-5

A catalogue of this publication is available from the British Library.

Published by Holroyd Publications
Sunderland

Printed by John Barry & Company Sunderland Tel: 0191 565 0748

Other titles by
John Ruttley
published by
Holroyd Publications.

Mowbray the people's Park

Acknowledgements,

I would like to thank James and Lisa McLeod for the assistance they have given me in the compiling of this book, and wish them well in their venture at Harperley. Also Dr Anthony Heller, an acknowledged expert on PoWs in Britain, who kindly supplied me with a lot of valuable information, and assisted with the translations of certain German words. The German ex-prisoners of war whom I met and interviewed- Rudi Lux, Paul Messer and Gerald Heyden. Colin Lea, the caretaker at the German Military Cemetery at Cannock Chase. Helen Pugh, at the London headquarters of the British Red Cross. Grant Mitchell, the senior archive officer at the International Federation of Red Cross and Red Crescent Societies Geneva. Martin Monger, and Fabrizio Bensi, at the International Committee of the Red Cross Geneva. Dr D. Bourgeois, and H. von Rutte, at the Swiss Federal Archives Geneva. Anita Atkinson editor, and the other staff of the Weardale Gazette. A. J. Williams, Head of Reader Information at the Public Record Office Kew. Denise Stones, Pamela Davies, and the other staff at Bishop Auckland Record Office. Liz Street at Staffordshire Record Office. The Commonwealth War Graves Commission. George Frazer, Regimental secretary Durham Light Infantry Museum. Mrs V. Bartlett, the Churchwarden at St James Hamsterley. Mrs S. Woods, Archivist Northumberland Record Office. Last but not least Miss J. Gill County Archivist, and the other staff at the Durham County Record Office, whose patience and expertise has helped me considerably in my research.

Introduction

In July 2002 the Arts Minister, Tessa Blackstone, following recommendations by English Heritage, announced that Harperley prisoner of war camp in County Durham had been granted Scheduled Monument status, the only PoW camp to be so honoured.

Dr Simon Thurtey, Chief Executive of English Heritage said, "The survival of Harperley is remarkable and extremely unusual- Harperley has an important wartime story to tell, and as an educational resource has enormous potential."

The camp's owners James and Lisa McLeod, working with English Heritage, are opening the camp to the public as a museum and visitor's centre. Their aim is 'to bring this important episode of 20th century history to life for the greater understanding of future generations'.

But there is even more to the fascinating story of Harperley than was realised at the time. The author has uncovered startling evidence that shows the camp has an even more terrible, traumatic, and tragic history than was originally thought.

Another sort of camp.

I first became aware that there used to be a prisoner of war camp near Hamsterley Forest in County Durham, while I was at scout camp there in the early 1960s. The Sunderland Sea Scout group I belonged to used to camp at a farm near Bedburn. My seven days at the campsite were really enjoyable; despite having some terrible inconveniences forced upon us young lads by the scout leaders. Such inconveniences as walking a mile each way to and from the village to buy bread every day. Taking turns to cook and wash up after each meal, and the appalling deprivations of having to carry our drinking water to the camp from the farm some distance away. The milk was collected from another farm up the hill, towards High Shipley, and this was even further away.

These experiences impacted on a boy born and bred in a large industrial town, and really made a lasting impression. I remember particularly having been very careful to avoid the large, livid looking bull, with the big metal ring in its nose, that snorted through its nostrils while looking at us threateningly over the top of the stable door in the farmyard. And I remember leaping onto the fence, milk churn in hand, to keep well away from the wicked looking horns of the cattle as they were driven down the farm track past us. These were Longhorns, the kind of cattle that we'd only ever previously seen in cowboy films.

Despite all this, and notwithstanding the souvenir scar I picked up on my right forearm that required four stitches at Bishop Auckland Cottage Hospital, (a wound received from some stray barbed wire, not the bull, nor the cattle, which were entirely blameless), it really was an enjoyable experience. A whole week outside in the open-air. Of course being active all day out in the sunshine did us lads the world of good. The various activities organised for us used an awful lot of our energy, so that we all ate like lions and slept like logs. It turned out to be the one and only week that I ever spent under canvass in my entire life, and I still have very fond memories of those seven days in the summer of 1960. I think that it was the first time I'd been away from home, and it was the first time in my life that I experienced homesickness.

While at the camp, a group of us decided to go swimming, as we were told that there was a pool nearby. We set off for Hamsterley forest, carrying our 'cosies' wrapped in our towels, and we soon came upon an open-air swimming pool at the edge of the trees. The pool was full of green coloured water, with bits of foliage floating on the surface. It obviously hadn't been cleaned for quite some time, but we jumped right in, and were soon splashing about happily in the cold water. It wasn't long before we discovered that the pool boasted a plaque stating that it had been constructed by PoWs during the Second World War. These words brought a great deal of imaginative thoughts to the mind of a 12-year-old boy. Born three years after the war had ended, my only knowledge of the conflict had been gleaned from the adventure films I'd seen at the cinema, and from the stories of daring and heroic deeds, told in comics such as the Adventure and the Rover. For me to actually see proof of enemy personnel being here was amazing. The fact that real live enemy soldiers, who had fought against Britain during the war, had been here, in Hamsterley forest, and had even left a facility for us to enjoy, made a lasting impression on me.

I have since been back to the forest as an adult, but was bitterly disappointed, and thought that my memory was deceiving me, as I couldn't find any sign of the pool. I later discovered that it had been filled in.

Nearly 40 years after attending the scout camp, in 1999, I read a newspaper report that an old prisoner of war camp at Harperley, near Crook, was still in existence, and was up for sale. This renewed my interest, and a little research turned up some quite unexpected and intriguing information.

This book is dedicated to all the prisoners who were held in Harperley and in similar camps, and particularly to those 27 who died while imprisoned at Harperley.

Harperley

Harperley prisoner of war camp was built in 1942. It had smaller satellite camps or hostels at Bedburn near Hamsterley, High Spen near Rowlands Gill, Lanchester, Langton Grange near Staindrop, and Usworth near Sunderland. There were other main camps in Durham at Oaklands Emergency Hospital at Bishop Auckland, Wolviston Hall, Coxhoe Hall, Walworth Castle and West Boldon.

The Harperley camp, number 93, was set up on a field on the 470 acre farm at Harperley strictly as required to conform with the prevalent hygiene and health rules. These regulations ensured that there was adequate heating, lighting and washing facilities etc for the internees. Initially the camp consisted purely of tents, but the Italian prisoners who were originally imprisoned there soon erected more substantial buildings on the 18-acre site. Chosen to hold the prisoners because of its remoteness, the area around Harperley has been inhabited by man since antiquity. The hills and forests of east Durham are spotted with the remains of early Britain's hill forts and settlements.

When the camp was constructed there were almost 16,000 Italian prisoners of war in the country, but very few German prisoners were held in Britain. Even as late in the war as 1944 there were less than 2,000 German PoWs imprisoned here. Fearful of a German invasion, the British government had shipped off most of the prisoners to Canada, or the United States as soon as possible after their capture.

After the unconditional surrender of Italy in 1943, a lot of the Italians were moved out to lower security camps, (the one at Bedburn near Hamsterley, where the swimming pool, was constructed, was such a camp). They were also placed in hostels, or were even billeted semi-permanently with the local population. Their places in the camp were taken by an influx of German prisoners during 1945. About a quarter of a million were transferred here from Europe to replace the Italians who had been sent home.

The main Harperley camp contained around 60 huts including the British compound that housed the guards. There were administrative offices, a cookhouse, barber's shop, ablutions, shower, bath, drying rooms, and carpenter's workshops. The camp had its own dentist, and priest, a chapel, library with around 2000 books (mostly second-hand). It also had a theatre with a stage, orchestra pit, and tiered seating, which doubled as a cinema. There are stories of the prisoners cheering the weekly Pathe newsreels when Hitler or some other high-ranking Germans was shown, and booing Churchill's appearances with gusto.

The prisoners put on their own theatre shows, including Melodie Der Liebe, an operetta by Enz, amongst many others. A professional musician led the camp's 11-piece orchestra, and there were also visits from entertainers from other camps, such as Marionette groups, that put on shows for the inmates. The prisoner's even printed their own newspaper, 'Der Quell, meaning 'The Source.' They also apparently had kept their sense of humour, which was evident in a number of ways, including the painting of imitation, tied back curtains, on the windows of some of the huts.

One of the larger of the camp huts at Harperley, the mess hall where the men, up to 180 at a time, ate their meals, has a number of murals painted on the walls. They are of rural and hunting scenes in Bavaria, and were painted by one of the more creative prisoners during his confinement there. The murals depict a variety of domestic and wild animals including a stag, foals, foxes, sheep, and a game bird. There are also water scenes and a man in lederhosen.

One of the water scenes has been identified as an actual location on the river Rhine in Germany. It depicts the story of Lorelei, (similar to a tale in Homer's Odyssey) where legend has it that a mermaid, singing from rocks near the river bank, lured many sailors to their destruction by wrecking their ships on the rocks near a sharp bend in the river.

The paintings were, no doubt, a very agreeable reminder of the prisoner's homeland, and of more pleasant times, and enjoyed by all the prisoners. The paintings are still there, on the mess hall walls, but most need some restoration work doing to them.

The prisoner's had their own organisation, entirely separate from the British camp next door. The German soldiers, headed by the camp leader, Ernst Herrman, were allowed to organise and run their own affairs, with as little interference as possible from the British guards. The camp even had its own jail, with a number of separate cells. The German's enforced their own discipline on the 1200 or so internees in the camp, and ensured its smooth running. The prisoners at Harperley were exclusively non-commissioned officers or private soldiers.

Most of the captured German officers lived in entirely separate camps from the troops. They were kept in camps such as the one at Featherstone in Northumberland, and had their own, more comfortable quarters and eating arrangements. They were exempt from working under the terms of the Geneva Convention, and spent most of their time being re-educated, and attending lectures about democratic leadership, and other, similar subjects. It seems that the officers had a lot of time to improve their minds, as there were a total of four orchestras, and three theatres in Featherstone camp.

Officers were provided with special grants called Selbsteinkleiderzusch to enable them to obtain uniforms. This money was paid by the German army to the prisoner's next of kin in Germany, who bought material and then had the uniforms made up by tailors and sent to England.

Like Harperley, camp 18 at Featherstone had its own newspaper which was called 'Die Zeit am Tyne.' It was printed professionally on the presses of the Hexham Courant. The newspaper expressed it's German editor's philosophical opinions, and published comments such as- 'We are realistic enough to know what it means to lose two world wars in a time span of only 30 years. That we didn't despair lies in the belief of us not having lost the intellectual and moral powers, but in the power that lies in the responsibility for the future. This we feel stronger now than at any other time.'

These newspapers also contained camp news, sports items, educational features, culture and entertainment columns, and even very well drawn and funny cartoons.

The Conflict

A great deal of resentment had been felt by the Germans since the armistice of 1918. They considered that they hadn't been beaten in the First World War, but betrayed, and stabbed in the back by powerful international financiers. This resentment, coupled with the weight of the crippling surrender conditions imposed on the country by the victorious Allies, created the political conditions within Germany that allowed the Fascist Party ideology to incubate, grow and flourish. Violent unrest persisted throughout the 1920s as various factions, including the Nazis and the Communists, fought amongst themselves on the streets, culminating with Hitler's Nationalist Socialist Party taking power.

World War Two started on 1st September 1939, when Germany, who had gradually, but persistently, broken all the paralysing restrictions imposed on her by the Allies First World War peace treaties, invaded Poland.

The combatants, Germany, Italy and Japan, on one side, lined up against Great Britain and the Commonwealth countries, and France, who were later joined by America, and Russia, on the other. The conflict lasted six years and took the lives of an estimated 55 million men women and children, 20 million of them from Russia alone. A total of 60 million people were displaced in Europe as a result of the fighting and bombing raids. The war involved almost every country in the world in one way or another. Millions of soldiers, sailor, airmen, and civilians lost their lives on both sides. Whole cities and even large parts of countries were destroyed and laid waste.

During this conflict hundreds of thousands of prisoners of war were taken by both sides, and were held until the end of the war before being repatriated. They were generally held in camps built specifically for the purpose, in out of the way places, in the most remote parts of the countryside.

A sudden surge of prisoner's flowed into Britain after the Allied victory in North Africa in October and November 1942. Later victories, and the capture of even larger numbers of enemy soldiers, entailed the transportation of immense numbers of German prisoners directly to the United States of America, and Canada, where special camps had been built to house them. Some of the prisoners complained bitterly about this, as crossing the Atlantic Ocean by boat was very dangerous at the time, owing to the activity of German submarines attacking Allied shipping. There were many instances of the vessels in such convoys being torpedoed and sunk, with high levels of fatalities.

Originally 300 camps were built across Britain to accommodate the prisoners held here. A number of these PoW camps were built in the North of England. Especially designed for security rather than comfort, they were wooden huts grouped together around a central administration centre and parade ground, generally with a vegetable garden, football pitch and recreation area nearby.

As the numbers of prisoners increased in Britain, a welfare committee was soon set up to ensure the well being of the prisoners. It included such groups as the British Red Cross, the YMCA, and representatives of the various main religious organisations. The Welfare Committee organised the accumulation and distribution of various toiletries such as toothpaste, toothbrushes, and soap, to the prisoners who couldn't obtain these from their own camp canteens.

Generally the British authorities provided sufficient quantities of food and clothing for the vast majority of prisoners, but times were hard, and even the British civilians had very few luxuries. They were simply not available.

Red Cross Parcels.

The German Red Cross arranged for parcels to be sent to the prisoners here in Britain. The families of the prisoners made up parcels of foodstuffs themselves, then passed them to the German Red Cross, to be sent to the PoWs held in this country. Later in the war, when adverse conditions caused severe food restrictions to be imposed on the German civilian population, the German Red Cross themselves offered standard parcels of a certain weight, with two types of food. These parcels were called in German Typenpakete. As well as the food, they also generally contained some cigarettes, tobacco and toiletries.

Items absolutely prohibited from the parcels were anything at all that could conceivably be thought to assist the prisoners in any escape attempts. A lot of these banned items were obviously dangerous in the hands of any prisoners, and included such diverse items as alcohol, nail files, and tools such as metal saws, files and screwdrivers.

Banned were escape aids like maps, cameras, drawing pens, scissors, compasses, pocketknives, tin openers, field glasses and money. Also excluded were cigarette papers and cigarette holders, carbon paper, marking ink, stencils, notebooks and calendars, anything which could conceivably be used to forge documents such as identification cards and travel documents.

Certain sports equipment was also forbidden, obvious things such as, skis, metal golf clubs, dumb-bells and Indian clubs. But others such as whistles, tennis and ping-pong nets, tennis balls, gymnastic rings, boxing gloves, and football boots, found their way onto the forbidden list, even though they are not at all obviously useful to escapees trying to get back to their own country. However, someone in authority with a vivid imagination had obviously thought that they might be used that way.

In 1941, with the consent of the British government, the German Red Cross paid significant amounts of money to their representatives in Britain, who then bought and distributed Christmas gifts to the German prisoners. This occurred again in 1942, but in 1943 the shortage of luxury goods in this country was so severe, that the German Red Cross was asked by the British authorities to buy the presents abroad, and send them to Britain, instead of buying them here.

As well as food, the German Red Cross sent books, musical instruments, gramophone records, typed scripts of plays, and even reproductions of great works of art. They were of the opinion that the prisoner's continued education was very important. As early as 1941 they had sent questionnaires to all prisoners requesting information on each PoW's trade or profession. Armed with this information they then set about a comprehensive distribution of the relevant educational material to the camps. Prisoner's correspondence courses called Soldatenbrife were organised, and the curricula standardised. Examinations taken in the camps were marked by approved German Ministry of Education examining boards. Only the final university examinations couldn't be taken in the camps.

The larger camps offered not just academic subjects, but courses in practical things such as baking, cooking, carpentry, tailoring, cobbling, haircutting, gardening, motor mechanics, plumbing, painting and decorating. Most of the prisoners also wished to learn, or improve their English, and the language courses were very popular.

Work.

Keeping the prisoners occupied was an important task. The Geneva Convention forbade their use in any type of work that could be regarded as war work, that is, from any type of work that could conceivably be thought to be used to make war on their own countries. So they couldn't be utilised say, in an ammunition factory, or in the shipyards. They were usually employed on the land, repairing the roads, working in quarries, and on building sites. Another task often set for the prisoners was removing rubble strewn around after the bombing raids. The local farmers made great use of them for the routine farm labouring work in the fields, and for rebuilding dry stone walls.

Harperley was classified as a work camp, and most of the prisoners were kept busy on various projects, including working the land on the adjacent farms. Labourers were in short supply because of the war, and there was a great demand for food, so there were large amounts of work to complete. In theory the prisoners could refuse to work, but if they didn't work then they wouldn't get paid, and there would be no money to buy the little luxuries that make camp life more bearable, such as cigarettes and toothpaste.

The Women's Land Army was also employed to great effect on farms, compensating for the lack of male workers. This organisation was founded in 1916, during the First World War, specifically to organise female labour to work on farms, and it had 16,000 members by the end of 1918. It was formed again in 1943 and some 87,000 of its members were employed on the land in Britain, many of them working alongside German prisoners of war.

The prisoners were expected to work hard, but were paid reasonably well, and provided with clothes and food. They were paid a nominal wage for the work. This was paid to them in camp tokens, worth about five shillings a week, (25 pence), and this could only be spent in the camp canteen. The prisoners were forbidden any sort of British currency. Later, voluntary overtime was rewarded with credits that were accrued, and saved for the prisoners in accounts. These were available to be collected after the war, but only by presenting the British government cheques at Banks in Germany, after the prisoners had returned home.

PoW's labour was also used to great effect in less obvious ways. As well as the open-air swimming pool in Hamsterley forest, a flight of 300 steps cut into a steep wooded hillside at Richmond in North Yorkshire was another useful task completed by PoWs during the Second World War. The steps are still used daily by the local population taking their constitutionals. A plaque reminds today's grateful users of the steps of the hard work and effort of the prisoners who constructed them.

Other such reminders include a game larder built in a garden in Rothbury in Northumberland. In the days before refrigerators, these larders where the only way of storing meat for any length of time, and no doubt the larder was received with gratitude by the householder.

Utilising the labour of prisoners of war isn't exactly new. Captured enemy prisoners have been put to work by their captors throughout recorded history by the Greeks, Romans and many others. During the Napoleonic wars, in the early 1800's, a number of French PoW's labour was used by the British to widen the gap in the hill at Houghton-le-Spring in County Durham. They helped to form the 'Houghton Cut', and allowed a wider roadway to be built through the hilltop. This thoroughfare is still used today, and is part of the main A690 Sunderland to Durham road.

French PoWs were also used in the construction of a new lighthouse near the quayside at North Shields in 1808. The structure, called the Highlight, to distinguish it from the other lighthouse, the Lowlight on the quayside, was built by John Stokoe for the Masters and Mariners of Trinity House of Newcastle, and replaced an older light built in 1727. It is still standing today, and was recently converted into a unique dwelling house.

Being usefully employed in non-warlike tasks, which were nevertheless valuable to the local community, was no doubt therapeutic to the PoWs themselves. Although they were expected to work hard, it must have been somewhat of a relief for them to get out of the claustrophobic atmosphere of the camp at times, and to be actively and gainfully employed doing something useful.

Although treated reasonably well, and fed and clothed adequately (the German prisoners were given, the same rations as the British armed forces, and this was more than the civilian population received), the prisoners could hardly be described as content. Even in the very best of conditions, how could they be happy, or content, when most if not all of them, just wanted to return to their own countries and be reunited with their families.

These men had their world turned upside down, and of course must have wondered and worried about their wives, and families constantly.

Labour continued to be in desperately short supply for quite some time after the war had ended, and from the end of the war right up until 1950 the British government was recruiting voluntary workers abroad, including some 74,000 from Germany.

Many prisoners of war were forced by the British government, probably in defiance of the Geneva Convention; to be used in employment here long after the end of the war, until the last were repatriated in 1948. Some of these unwilling workers refused to be called prisoners of war and maintained that they were being used as forced labour, and should have been sent home a lot sooner.

The British government's attitude seemed to be that as the German's had caused most of the damage to this country with their bombing, and the labour shortage was caused by the fighting, then perhaps the German PoWs should be made to rectify some of the damage the war had caused.

However, this caution regarding the prisoner's repatriation was not wholly due to the British government's reluctance to lose its supply of labour, but also because Russia was still viewed with suspicion, and the possibility of rearming, and another conflict breaking out, was real.

The cold war between Russia and the west hadn't yet started, but all the ingredients were already there, mistrust, prevarication and hostility.

Apart form the politics, the very logistics required to repatriate some 400,000 men was awesome, especially so, considering the absolute confusion and turmoil that the whole of Europe, and especially Germany, was in immediately after the war. To repatriate that huge amount of men properly, needed careful planning and preparation. This was necessarily a time taking affair and couldn't be arranged overnight.

There was also the fact that quite a lot of PoWs didn't wish to return to their homes because where they had once lived was now under the direct control of the Russians. This was as a result of the treaty of Yalta, which was ratified at Potsdam, and agreed by the Allies as the war approached its conclusion. The treaty divided up large parcels of Europe between the Allies. The returning prisoners, being ex-German Army personnel, would almost certainly have been imprisoned, or worse by the Russians if they had returned home. Something over 25,000 prisoners, just over 6% of the total amount, stayed here in Britain after the war, and almost 800 married local girls (as did some of the camp's British guards).

One of the better known German ex-prisoners who stayed behind was Bert Trautmann. Bert stayed in England after the war and volunteered for bomb disposal work. Eventually becoming a professional footballer, he was goalkeeper for Manchester City, and played in goal for the team during the 1956 FA Cup final. He broke his neck making a spectacular save in the goalmouth during the game. Bert played on for the remaining 17 minutes of the match despite being in great pain. It was later discovered that he'd broken five vertebrae his neck and he spent the next six months in plaster. Other ex-prisoners were not so well known outside of their local communities, but nevertheless still contributed much to their adopted country.

Rudi Lux.

One of these ex-prisoners is Rudi Lux. At 16 years old he was already a member of the Home Guard in his home town of Massow in Germany, (now a part of Poland), and he volunteered to join the 11th Panzer Grenadier Division (Nordland), a motorised SS regiment. Rudi reasoned that he would have a better chance of escaping the fast approaching Russian Army if he were with a motorised unit.

Rudi was only a serving soldier for six weeks before being taken prisoner by the Americans near Schwerin on 2nd May 1945. His regiment went out of their way to surrender to the Americans, rather than be taken prisoner by the Russians. He was held in a makeshift camp, just tents erected in the forest, before being handed over to the British. The prisoners were taken to a German concentration camp near Hamburg and imprisoned there for two days. Here Rudi saw the appalling conditions inside the camp at first hand, and he thinks the Allies placed them in the camp to make a point. The were then transported to Hanover, then Munster, and then to a camp at Fallingbostel, an ex- PoW camp for Allied prisoners, where they were held for six months. The conditions in the camp were terrible. After a number of further moves, Rudi was taken to England.

He was held briefly as a prisoner at Harperley camp before being moved to Darras Hall PoW camp in Northumberland. As Rudi describes in his book, from Pomerania to Ponteland, he was at first suspected of being a dangerous Nazi after his capture because he was a member of an SS regiment. It was only after a number of lengthy interviews with German speaking Home Office interrogators, that he was finally reclassified as a 'Grey' prisoner, which meant that they realised that he wasn't at all interested in politics, and was free of the fanatical Nazi mentality.

The SS or Schutz Staffeln was German for Protection Squads. The regiment was formed as a personal bodyguard for Hitler in 1925, and Hendrick Himmler became its head or Reichsfurhrer in 1929. Originally it had 300 members, but within four years of being taken over by Himmler it had expanded to over 50,000.

To gain membership of the regiment initially, special criteria were required. Prospective members of the prestigious elite guard, which was also the leading Paramilitary force in Germany, had to be tall, blond and be able to trace their pure Aryan ancestry in a straight line right back at least to the year 1750. As the Nazi party's strength and influence grew so did the demand from the German upper classes to join.

By 1937 all three major concentration camps in Germany were run by the SS Totenkopfverbande or Deaths Head units, which also performed State Police duties.

In 1938 the regiment formed a 200,000 strong Action Group or Verfugungstruppe. This later became the Waffen, or Military SS. Membership rose quickly to 240,000 by the end of 1938. Later, near the end of the war membership soared to reach one million.

Shortages of men forced the Germans to organise the formation of other regiments, which, although called SS, bore no resemblance to the notorious Deaths Head squads staffing the concentration camps. These newly

25

formed regiments were destined to be sent to fight in the appalling conditions at the Russian front. It was to one of these units that Rudi Lux had volunteered to join at the age of 16.

Rudi only spent a matter of weeks at Harperley camp, and while there was transported on the back of a lorry every day to the sea front at Roker in Sunderland. He was put to work there helping to remove large concrete anti-tank blocks from the beach, which were part of the coastal defences against possible invasion.

After being transferred to the camp at Darras Hall in Northumberland, he worked on farms in that area. He particularly remembers two of the most popular tunes of that time, Give Me Five Minutes More, and The Woody Woodpecker Song, which were played over the camp's tannoy system repeatedly.

He later worked, and was billeted, at the Hospital farm at St Mary's mental hospital near Morpeth, were he had the dubious distinction of having his very own padded cell next to his bedroom.

After his release in 1948 Rudi married a local girl and remained in England. He did a lot valuable work as a youth leader in Widdrington in Northumberland for 17 years before he retired.

Gerald Heyden

Gerald Heyden was imprisoned in Harperley for about 12 months. His was captured by the Canadians in Northern France near Caen, where the British had invaded, in July 1945, only a month after the D-Day landings.

Gerald was born in Schwerin in Mecklenburg, in eastern Germany. Like most of the other German children of the period, Gerald was a member of the various Youth movements such as the Falcons, and joined the Jungvolk, the junior Hitler Youth, when he was about ten years old. He remembers doing a lot of marching and singing, but thinks their activities were not much different from those engaged in by the British Boy Scouts. There were two sessions a week, each lasting two hours, on Wednesday and Saturday afternoons.

After leaving school he went to teacher training college, joining the Army after taking his exams. He joined a crack Panzer regiment in the summer of 1943, and exactly a year later was in England, as a PoW.

Soon after his capture he was transported across the English Channel to Southampton in a landing craft, along with other captives He was formally interrogated at Hampton Court, then sent on the long train journey to a camp in Comrie, near Perth in Scotland.

He wasn't in Scotland for very long before setting sail from the Clyde on the New Amsterdam, a liner carrying thousands of German prisoners to America. The ship was very crowded, and Gerald remembers having to find a place to sleep wherever he could on the floor. There were three sittings at every meal, and a fair amount of food was served on board, but most of it reappeared during the stormy

Atlantic crossing.

The prisoners disembarked at New York, no doubt very pleased to be on dry land again, and then spent two days on a train travelling across the country to the central American State of Kansas. They were employed there on the land, then in Nebraska, and in Michigan, working in factories, sugar refining plants, and picking crops of tomatoes and maize.

The atmosphere seems to have been fairly relaxed. Local farmers would call at the camp and pick up three or four prisoners in their cars, and drive them to the farms. They worked hard, but were treated well, even eating with the farmer's families. The smaller PoW camps were not even fenced in. The prisoner's were given American army uniforms that had POW stencilled in large letters on the backs of the tunics.

In February 1946, after working in America for six months, the prisoners were again marched onto a ship and told that they were going home. They landed in Belgium, but didn't go home, instead they were quickly returned to England, where there was still a desperate shortage of labour. They were given English battle dress uniforms with holes cut in the backs of the tunics and the knees of the trousers, where brightly coloured pieces of cloth was sown to distinguish them as prisoners. They were taken to Stansted, then Bury St Edmunds, and then to Aldershot, were Gerald worked in the army garrison bakery, helping to bake 25,000 loafs of bread every shift.

He arrived in Harperley early in 1947, marching from the railway station at Crook to the camp, and was given work that summer making hay and reaping the harvest on the surrounding farms. He also worked in Hamsterley forest where a great number of trees were then just being planted. He helped to divert the course of the stream at Bedburn, and used stones to lay roads into the forest. During the winter, when there was little work on the farms to keep them occupied, the prisoners were taken up Weardale by truck, to a quarry near Ireshopeburn, where they quarried stone that was then sent to the furnaces of Redcar Steel Works. At other times when there wasn't much work to do, they stayed in camp and made children's toys, carved wooden ornaments, and made leather goods such as carpet slippers stuffed with sacks, which they sold to the local population. These were especially popular around Christmas time.

He remembers that there were a variety of recreational pursuits, including the playing of musical instruments, and watching shows performed by theatre groups in the camp. Education was actively encouraged, and a number of various classes were very popular with the prisoners, and well attended. The local Salvation Army band often visited the camp on Saturday mornings, and their music was always well received.

Gerald made friends with some of the local population, and didn't come across any nastiness or hatred. He remembers that the general sentiment of the locals was that they hoped that their relatives would have been treated in the same manner, had they been captured in Germany. He worked for a while at Langton Grange near Staindrop, which was one of Harperley's smaller satellite camps.

29

The official relaxing of the non-fraternisation rule at the end of 1946, meant that the prisoner's could mix freely with the locals, and go to dances which were well attended and popular with the local girls. Gerald remembers making a nocturnal date with a local girl, but thought better of it, and didn't turn up, rather than risk climbing the wire surrounding the camp and breeching the camp security.

He made fiends with many locals, especially the blacksmith Mr Dawson and his family at Thornley, near Tow Law, and visited them regularly.

Gerald married a local girl in November 1948 while still technically a prisoner of war, and still required to report to the police once a week. His wife's mother wasn't happy about her daughter marrying a prisoner of war, and refused to attend the wedding. Her mother didn't speak to Gerald's wife for six months after the wedding, but then came around and accepted the situation. She soon got to know, and to like Gerald. Ironically, he discovered that his wife's brother had been a prisoner in Germany, having being shot down during an air raid over Nuremburg in 1942 while serving with Bomber Command. He had jumped from his blazing plane, parachuted to safety, and luckily he was immediately taken prisoner by the German Police who then handed him over to the Army. If he'd have been captured by the civilians he might have received far rougher treatment, because understandably, they didn't think a lot of the allied airmen who were bombing their city, and causing so much destruction.

He was imprisoned in the notorious Stalag Luft 111, and took part in the famous great escape in March 1944, but was one of those who were captured before managing to get clear of the camp, and spent ten days in solitary confinement as punishment. The escape, (immortalised in the 1663 film 'The Great Escape', starring Steve McQueen and Richard Attenborough), coincided with a huge Allied bombing raid on Berlin, and Hitler was so enraged that he personally ordered 50 of the recaptured escapees to be shot.

Gerald, recently recruited by the German army, was on guard duty near Brussels in Belgium at the time. He remembers that he was warned to keep a strict watch for any of the 76 escapees, little realising that his future brother-in-law was one of the prisoners attempting to escape, and that within a year or so, he would be a prisoner himself, in England.

Gerald choose to remain after being released, and has lived here contentedly ever since. His father was taken from Germany to Siberia when his hometown came under Russian control after the war. Transported with a lot of the other males over 18 years of age, they were forced to build the new towns there. His father, and countless others, never returned.

Some of his family fled to the west in 1962, when the Berlin wall separating the East from the West, was erected. The wall effectively stopped people passing freely from one side to the other, and Gerard visited his family in West Germany. He returned to his home, now a part of a united Germany again, in 1995, after the wall had come down, and was reunited with some of his cousins that he hadn't seen for 52 years.

Paul Messer.

Another ex-prisoner still living in England is Paul Messer. Paul's story is typical of so many of that period, and he has very strong links with the northeast, and is now living in Morpeth,

Mr Messer was born in Duisburg north West Germany, and was serving with a parachute regiment when he was captured by the American forces, while retreating after the Allied invasion of northern France. This was in September 1944, just seven days before his 18th birthday. Their Commanding officer, a major who was reported to be friendly with Herman Goring the high ranking Nazi, shot himself in the head immediately after negotiating his unit's surrender. This was a very great shock to Paul and the other members of the unit.

The prisoners were loaded onto a train to be taken to a camp near Le Harve. Ironically, the camp had previously held French PoWs captured by the Germans. They were on the train for two days, 50 men to a carriage, and given only old meat to eat. Their only sanitation was two buckets filled with water they were given to wash themselves with. The men ripped up a couple of the floorboards in the train carriage, and decided to use the narrow gap in the floor as a toilet. During a brief stop, Paul, and some others, decided to widen the gap even further and make their escape. He and a group of another four prisoners made their get away, intending to head for the South of France, where they had heard there was a possibility they could get a train back to Germany.

They made good their escape. This was during October and November, and the weather was very cold, but they lived off the land, eating whatever fruits and berries they could find.

A farmer eventually found them sleeping in a haystack. Although obviously very hungry, and suffering from the effects of sleeping rough, the farmer didn't offer them any food, but handed them over to the police, who then promptly turned them over to the American soldiers again. They were redirected back to the PoW camp, and kept in the recovery section for a couple of days, where they were given special rations to bring their body weight back to its normal level.

Eventually they were taken to the docks at Le Harve, where they boarded a ship, crossed the English Channel, and joined a large convey of ships at Southampton, and then sailed to America. The prisoners were well fed on the ship, and Paul wasn't troubled at all by seasickness.

After landing safely in New York, they were transported by train to a large camp holding 20,000 men at Camp Forrest, Tullahoma. Tennessee. The prisoners were put to work making what they were told were fishing nets, but the PoWs were convinced they were going to be used as camouflage netting.

Paul decided to escape again, and intended to head for Florida, where he'd heard that there were a lot of German speaking Americans who might help him. Paul, together with a colleague, managed to climb the high wire fence and they made their getaway. Wearing a couple of old greatcoats over their instantly recognisable prisoner's uniforms, they were alarmed when they discovered that their photographs were in all the local newspapers, and that their descriptions were being broadcast repeatedly by the radio stations.

Eventually, after a couple of days of avoiding capture, they chanced hitching a life from a passing motorist. The driver stopped, but their initial relief at getting a lift soon turned to disappointment when he pulled a gun on them, and drove then to the nearest town, where he handed them into the sheriff's office at gun point. Returned to the camp, Paul was given 30 days solitary confinement on bread and water as punishment. The punishment was eased a little with the proviso that he received a hot meal every four days.

It was while he was in solitary confinement that his older brother Josef arrived in the camp. His brother had been captured while serving in the Afrika Korps under Field Marshal Rommel, and it was only by chance that he had learned of Paul's imprisonment in the camp, seeing his brother's name on the notice board listing his punishment for the escape attempt. They could have remained in such a large camp, with such a huge amount of prisoners for years, each never knowing that the other was there.

His punishment complete, and reunited with his brother, Paul settled into camp life. He worked at the variety of different tasks he was allocated. Most of them were mind numbingly boring, particularly the harvesting of peanuts in Alabama. Paul remembers that even harvesting peanuts paled into insignificance compared to picking cotton in Mississippi. This was the most difficult and painful work that he had ever experienced. Filling countless numbers of nine-foot long sacks, with the fluffy cotton buds, while trying to avoid the prickly stalks, was difficult, and very painful.

One day they were shown a film in the camp. It was taken in a concentration camp in Germany, and showed the horrors of the inmate's mistreatment. The prisoners at first refused to believe that such things were happening in their homeland, and thought that the film was a forgery made by the Allies, but eventually they had to accept the stark truth that the film was indeed genuine. The revelation was a great shock to the prisoners; they were totally unaware of such things going on in those camps.

In early 1946 Paul was shipped back to England. He became separated from his brother again while they were on the jetty waiting to board the boats, Paul boarding one, and Josef being marched aboard an entirely different ship.

When they arrived in England, their new British commanding officer thought that the prisoners had been spoiled, and fed far too much by the American's. They were all immediately put on a strict diet of bread, jam, and water to compensate for their supposed overfeeding.

They were taken to a Camp at Bury St Edmunds first, then to Sennybridge in Wales. Paul volunteered to work in the cookhouse, and was eventually given work in the officer's mess. After a year in Wales he was moved to Rugley in Staffordshire, where, after being finally demobbed in March 1948, he met and married his first wife Helen.

He went back to his hometown of Duisburg after being released, but soon came back to England, and worked in the priority industries of mining and agriculture initially, before moving to catering work as a chef.

While working for Glassier Metal Company he met Irene, a girl from the northeast, whom also worked for the company as the works canteen manageress. By now divorced from his first wife, he subsequently married Irene, who introduced him to the north east region. They settled here permanently, and lived here happily, despite Paul's initial difficulties with understanding the Geordie accent.

After the war.

Because some of the prisoners were forced to stay on in Britain after the end of hostilities, the new interim German government introduced extra measures to compensate the prisoners still held here. They paid them an additional two German Marks a day after 1st January 1947, which increased to 5 Marks a day after 1st January 1949.

It was estimated that in 1946 there were 400,000 German prisoners in this country, including 127,000 transported here from the USA and Canada, as the threat of invasion receded.

Kempton racecourse, and other, equally improbable venues were used as reception centres to process the thousands of German prisoners transferred to Great Britain. It was calculated that up to 20% of the total British workforce working on the land were PoWs. Others worked on roads and building sites, and for the Forestry Commission. At the time almost every town in Britain had its own PoW camp, of one type or another. There were eventually about 15,000 camps spread across the country. A multitude of old mills; factories, manor houses, and army camps were converted to hold the captured enemy personnel.

Local priests and ministers would take services of divine worship in the camps. Sometimes the prisoners would be allowed to visit the local parish church and attend services alongside the local congregation, the hymn sheets being typed in both English and German. One hymn that was always very popular with the prisoners was 'Glorious Things Will Be Outspoken' and is actually the tune of

German National Anthem with different words. Fraternisation with the prisoners was strictly forbidden until the end of 1946, and the Germans would leave the church before the service ended to avoid mingling with, and making any contact at all with the civilian population.

On December 12th 1946 the ban on fraternisation was lifted, and this had a profound effect of the prisoner's morale. Local choirs visited some of the camps at Christmas, and prisoners were invited into the homes of the local civilian population who offered them hospitality. Presents were exchanged, and toys made by the PoWs were given to children.

The relaxation of the non-fraternization rule had a big impact on the prisoners in a lot of ways. The prisoners at Harperley could now even play 'international' football against Crook town AFC, and games were organised against other PoW camps. Table tennis games were played against English players, and even chess tournaments, and athletic events were organised. The prisoners, although still living in the camps, could now visit the local pubs and clubs, and attend dances and social evenings. Attitudes on both sides changed as the prisoners became a familiar sight in the area, and got to know the locals.

The 1947 Christmas edition of the Harperley camp newspaper, Der Quell, contained short stories and poetry. It reported that the winter weather was the worst on record, and that a Miss Hawthorn had recently given a lecture to the prisoners on the subject 'The role of women in English life'.

Lieutenant Colonel Stobart

The prisoner of war camps were all well guarded, and security was always paramount. But after the end of the war, at Harperley, it was more of a sensible, balanced surveillance. The camp was run in the most efficient and humane manner possible, with the need for security coupled with the equally important needs of the prisoners as human beings. The camp was as self-sufficient, and as self-contained as possible.

The British commander at Harperley, Lieutenant Colonel Stobart, seemed to have a very liberal attitude towards the prisoners, which appeared to work well.

Lieutenant Colonel George Kinnear Stobart OBE, DL, JP, served in the Durham Light Infantry, and took over as Commandant of Harperley from Major Tetlow, when the Major retired. Colonel Stobart was educated at Wellington College, and at the Royal Military College, Sandhurst, where he was his classes prize cadet. Stobard's family owned Harperley Hall, next door to the camp, and his private residence was at Helme Park, just a short distance away, where he lived with his wife.

Joining the regiment in 1921, he served with the First Battalion of the Durham Light Infantry in Upper Silesia, and then with the King's African Rifles in Uganda from 1925 to 1930. He joined the Second Battalion in India in 1930, eventually taking command in 1941. Injured in Africa, he took over as commandant at Harperley in 1945 on his return to England.

Colonel Stobart was held in high regard by his fellow officers, and it was said of him that he radiated integrity, and was a living example of the ideal qualities befitting an officer and a gentleman. He was instrumental in the forming of a DLI Memorial Garden in the College at Durham Cathedral, and in all the work that led to the Regimental Chapel appearing as it does today.

The Colonel encouraged the prisoners to attend Classes in Maths, Physics, and English Literature, which were given by visiting lecturers from Durham University. A total of 18 guest speakers of various nationalities came to the camp and spoke on a wide variety of subjects including politics, economics and religion. A Dr Bauer even debated the possibility of a European Union, a concept which although having being actually realised today, is still the subject of a lot of very heated debate. There were also regular visits by some of the prisoners to the library at Durham University. The prisoners attended Council meetings, Labour Party meetings, and studied political history at the Worker's Education Association at Crook. Indeed the camp life seems to have been made tolerable at least, if not pleasant. The attitude of the British guards, and the local population, seemed to be remarkably friendly.

Even though a lot of the prisoners had little knowledge of what was happening to their relatives back in Germany, morale was generally high under the Colonel's enlightened rule except, apparently, during screening. Each prisoner was screened, and given a grade between Black, White or Grey. The White's being considered the lowest security risk, and the Black's the highest. Most of the prisoners at Harperley were in the low risk category, being White's and Grey's,

The Commandant's office. Lieutenant Colonel Stobart's hut in the camp.

The theatre in Harperley Camp, with orchestra pit and tiered seating.

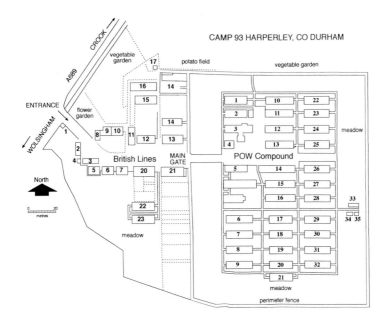

Plan of the camp at Harperley, supplied by Dr Anthony Hellens to accompany his articles in the Weardale Gazette, and reproduced here with his kind permission. The map is based on the official camp plan of June 26th 1946, redrawn by F. G. Hickey in 1991. This simplified version was redrawn by Ann Rooke, Geography Dept. University of Newcastle.

Camp 93 (Harperley Camp), Crook, Co. Durham
Camp Buildings - Main Functions:

BRITISH LINES

1. Guard Room
2. Garage
3 - 4. Cycle Sheds
5. Carpenter's Shop
6. Labour Office
7. Quartermaster's Stores
8-10. Sergeant's Hut, Mess and Cookhouse
11. Cookhouse
12. Tailor's Workshop
13. Office & Interpreter
14. Detention Cells
15. Sleeping Quarters
16. PANA
17. Painter's Shop
18. Switch House
19. Lavatories
20. Switch House
21. Lavatories
22. Stores & Admin Office
23. Offices/Adjutant's and CO's Office
24. Officers' Mess
25. Officers' Quarters
26. Greenhouse

POW COMPOUND

1. Compound Office
2. Store Room
3. Cookhouse
4. Barber's Shop
5. Camp Reception Station
6-9. Sleeping Quarters
10. Dining Hut
11. Theatre
12. Dining Hut
13. Canteen
14. Showers, Bath and Drying Room
15-17. Ablutions
18-20. Sleeping Quarters
21. Church
22-32. Sleeping Quarters
33-35. Carpenter's Workshops

The remaining original camp buildings at Bedburn in Hamsterley Forest today.

The field at Shipley Moss where the First World War prison camp was built.
The clump of bushes in the bottom right corner is where the remains of the filter bed are.

The circular brick filter bed, the only visible remains of the First World War camp.

Some of the quarry workings on Knitsley Fell, where the prisoners worked.

The twelfth century church of St James' Hamsterley.

The churchyard of St James' Hamsterley, where the 27 deceased prisoners were buried.

Gerald Heyden in
German Army Uniform

Gerald Heyden today

Paul Messer in
German Paratrooper's
uniform. He escaped
twice while a PoW

Paul Messer today

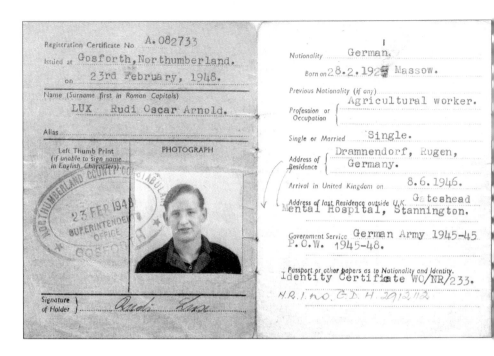

Registration Certificate No. A. 082733

Issued at Gosforth, Northumberland.

on 23rd February, 1948.

Name (Surname first in Roman Capitals)
LUX Rudi Oscar Arnold.

Alias

Left Thumb Print
(if unable to sign name
in English Characters).

PHOTOGRAPH

Signature
of Holder

Nationality .... German.

Born on 28.2.192? Massow.

Previous Nationality (if any)

Profession or
Occupation { Agricultural worker.

Single or Married .... Single.

Address of
Residence { Dramnendorf, Rugen,
Germany.

Arrival in United Kingdom on 8.6.1946.

Address of last Residence outside U.K. Gateshead
Mental Hospital, Stannington.

Government Service German Army 1945-45
P.O.W. 1945-48.

Passport or other papers as to Nationality and Identity.
Identity Certificate WO/NR/233.

H.R.I.no.G.D.H.2912112

Above:
Rudi Lux's prisoner of war identity card showing his discharge date of 23rd February 1948. He still had to report to the police as an alien until 1961

Right:
Rudi Lux today

with only 30% being classified as Black's, which included SS men, and fervent Nazis. Generally, whenever possible, most of these higher grades of prisoners were transferred to more secure camps, along with captured U-Boat, and Luftwaffe crews.

Many of the older prisoners disagreed with the official German government propaganda, and despised the Nazis outlook and principles. However, some of the younger ones were more stubborn, and resisted efforts made to rehabilitate them. They preferred to make trouble whenever they could by trying to disrupt camp life, and by refusing to cooperate with the authorities.

At the end of the war, the prisoners were gradually repatriated to their homelands. The lowest graded White's first, then the others in stages. The government tried to re-educate and 'de Nazi' the most fervently brainwashed and indoctrinated prisoners before repatriating them back to Germany. These were generally the younger men who had been indoctrinated at school or while members of the Hitler Youth, or other such youth organisations in Germany before they had joined the army.

It was during this period that some of the prisoner's wives travelled from Germany and visited the camp, and at least one open day was held, and proved to be a great success.

Going Home.

By the winter of 1946, the British government announced that around 15,000 prisoners a month were being sent home, but some cynics allege that the men were simply being moved to different camps around the country, and were still being employed here. However, some 257,000 prisoners had definitely been returned to Germany by the end of 1947. However a further 24,000 or so remained here, and didn't wish to be sent back. They requested six month long extensions to remain, which were granted by the British government. When the six months were up they requested a further six month extension, and so on. A lot of these men met, and married British girls, and settled permanently in this country. Others completed their education here before returning to Germany

The camp at Harperley finally closed in 1948, after the last of the prisoners was repatriated. Colonel Stobart retired from the army and joined Northern Forestry Products. The camp huts were then briefly used for housing Polish refugees, and later as a police hostel. When the owner, Charley Johnson, resumed occupation of the Harperley site soon after, he refused the government's offer to demolish the camp, not because of any reasons of sentimentality, but for purely practical purposes, preferring to utilise the huts for the storage of his animal feed, fertilisers, and farm machinery.

Mr Johnson died in 1999, and the site is now owned by James and Lisa McLeod, who live on the other side of the valley, at Bracken Hill Farm. They have rejuvenated the buildings, and are opening the camp as a museum and visitor's centre, with the assistance of English heritage.

The McLeod's lost all their stock in the foot and mouth culls in 2001, and are determined to make a go of their new enterprise. Naturally the main subjects are the prisoner's held during the Second World War, but each hut has a different theme. They have put in a great deal of hard work by clearing the undergrowth, and the six-foot high brambles that once blocked the pathways through the camp.

They have recently come into possession of photographs of the theatre group that played in the camp's theatre, have copies of some of the operetta music scores, and have met some of the ex- prisoners, who have travelled from Germany to revisit the camp.

The camp has a pleasant atmosphere, and is in effect a time capsule, an interesting and informative place to visit now that the McLeod's have completed their hard work. Its position, at the head of the Wear valley, on the A689 road from Crook to Wolsingham, is ideally situated, right at the entrance to Weardale, and is attracting many visitors.

At this point I thought that my research was complete and the Harperley story had ended. However information sent to me by the Swiss Federal Archives regarding details of a report by the International Committee of the Red Cross in Geneva, who I'd written to earlier, threw new light on the camp's history. It revealed a fascinating and tragic new aspect of the PoWs at Harperley, and opened up an entirely whole new dimension of the story for me.

Harperley- 1916

The information from the Swiss Federal Archives surprised me. I'd requested information regarding Harperley PoW camp from the International Red Cross, and if anything; I expected copies of any inspection reports that had been made by the Red Cross during the 1940's.

The International Federation of Red Cross and Red Crescent Societies informed me that it was founded in 1919, after the First Word War ended, and therefore held no records proceeding that date. They suggested that I approach its predecessor, the League of Red Cross Societies, which might hold copies of reports of visits. This I did, and they did indeed hold copies of two separate inspection visits to camps in Britain, these were conducted in January and December 1915. The camps visited were at Hollypoint and Dryffryn in North Wales. Doncaster, Donnington Hall, Firth Hill, Handforth and Leigh. I discovered later that Harperley camp was dependent upon Leigh, but it wasn't included in these inspections.

The Red Cross had kindly forwarded my request to the Swiss Federal Archive, also based in Geneva, and they sent me copies of the two inspection reports at Harperley that they held. However the copies of the reports they sent me were not dated 1940 something, but surprisingly were dated 1918.

The information contained in the reports, and the very fact that there was a camp at Harperley during the First World War came as a complete revelation to me.

The inspection reports revealed that there was a prisoner of war camp constructed at Harperley during the First World War. It was much smaller that its successor, containing only about 230 prisoners. The first German prisoners were transported by train on the Wear Valley Line to Harperley Station. The railway station is shown on the 1924 Ordinance Survey map, to be on the north side of the river Wear, just below Low Harperley farm.

At first the prisoners lived in tents in a field at Low Harperley farm, until more permanent wooden huts could be built at Shipley Moss, a site across the river Wear. There is still a narrow foot bride over the Wear at Low Harperley. The present bridge is obviously a fairly new steel structure, and has replaced its older predecessors. There is no obvious sign of any remaining Harperley Station buildings, the station cottages, or the Chapel shown on the 1924 Ordinance Survey Map, but the railway line is still there, although it isn't now operational. The passenger service was a casualty of the Beeching Report of 1963, but goods were still carried on the line until the closure of the Weardale cement works.

The permanent camp was near the farm at Shipley Moss, on the south side of the river, about a mile away from the site of Harperley Station. To reach the farm on foot is a testing uphill walk, but there is no other option, there is no vehicular access from this direction. The camp was supplied almost entirely by rail, and the prisoners were obliged to carry all their supplies up from the station.

Very little of the camp now remains. The only visible evidence of any structure is part of the circular brick wall of the filter bed, which was used as part of the latrine system. The filter bed stands forlornly in a corner of the featureless field, covered in rough undergrowth, with a sparse sprinkling of silver birch. The stream that once supplied the prisoners with fresh drinking water still flows down the sloping meadow, but now is only of interest to the grazing sheep. The soil underfoot in the camp field is firm enough, but the land surrounding the site of the camp has poor drainage, and is water sodden, making walking heavy going and progress difficult.

Past the farm, and higher still, perched on the summit of the windswept moor, are the remains of Knitsley Fell quarry. This is where the prisoners were employed to quarry a type of stone called ganister. It must have been an inhospitable place to work, especially in the winter months, toiling laboriously at their allocated tasks for days, weeks and years. Untidy piles of waste and slag, now overgrown with moss and grass, scar the skyline. The depressions are water filled, and the whole site looks bleak and depressing.

When the prisoners were employed here there was an overhead conveyer belt system running from the quarry, down the hill, over the top of Shipley Moss farm, and Bracken Hill farm. This structure carried the stone from the quarry right down to the railway line on the other side of the river, where it was transported away by train. There are still some remains of these concrete structures on the other side of the road from the quarry, where the farm track emerges, and in the field next to where the camp was situated. The whole area has a somewhat desolate appearance, and is littered with the remains of old quarry and mine workings. The place has obviously been a hive of industrial activity at various times in the past, and there were once even brickworks on the Fell.

The First World War.

The First World War started at midnight on the 4th August 1914 when German troops marched through Belgium to attack France, following the assassination of Arch Duke Ferdinand in Serbia. The British had signed a treaty with Belgium in 1839, which guaranteed its neutrality. The British government also had an agreement with France signed in 1904, and so came to the defence of its Allies when the German's mobilised their troops.

The commonwealth forces of Canada, Australia, New Zealand, and South Africa, backed Britain, and entered the conflict. By the end of the war a number of other countries including Russia, Portugal and the United States of America, were all fighting with the British against the Germans, and their Austria-Hungary alliance.

During the four years of bitter fighting that followed, there were many battles at sea, and on the Eastern, and Western fronts. Gallipoli, Jutland, Mons Verdun, Ypres, the Somme, Arras, and Passchendale being some of the best known. The fighting was fierce and bloody, and many men were killed and wounded on both sides, and a lot were captured. The German prisoners were quickly taken away from the front line by their captors, and incarcerated in secure camps around Britain until the end of the hostilities. Such a camp was at Harperley in County Durham.

As the war progressed and casualties multiplied, propaganda was used with great effect by both sides, and inflamed public opinion. For a time suspicion and hostility against anyone with a foreign accent in this country was rife. This was not just aimed at the newly arrived German prisoners of war, but against the existing German population living in Britain. Many German civilians were put in interment camps until the end of hostilities. The general feeling was that it was better to be safe than sorry, and the fact that thousands of aliens in the country were rounded up and grouped together where they could do no harm seemed to be universally desired.

The Allies had opened a new major offensive on the Somme on the 8th August 1918, and although the going was very hard, they made some progress against the seriously weakened and outnumbered enemy. With the assistance of the French and an influx of fresh American troops, their initial slow advance turned almost into a virtual routing of the German forces. The opposing sides had become bogged down in the ineffective trench warfare that only ever succeeded in blocking the other side's advances. No major gains or losses of ground had been accomplished by either side in years. This time it was different. The Allies pressed forward their determined advance and made great inroads into the territory previously held by the Germans.

Another great victory was announced at Ypres on 2nd October. The fighting had commenced on 26th September and this, the fourth battle for the same ground, finally ended a week later. The whole of the German defensive lines on the front were beginning to crumble, and there were lots of rumours that the war was about to end.

The morale of the German soldiers was very low, and things started to go even more disastrously wrong very quickly. Ludendorff, the German Army's Quartermaster General, and Chief of Staff to Hindenburg, resigned on 27th

October, to avoid being dismissed.

Worsening conditions on their warships resulted in the German fleet mutinying on the 29th October, causing great unrest throughout the rest of the German forces, and on 30th October Germany's principal collaborator Turkey, signed an armistice with the Allies. The coalition was crumbling. The Austria-Hungary Empire soon followed, and signed an armistice on 3rd November. The Kaiser, Wilhelm the 2nd, the King of Germany, abdicated and fled the country to live in exile in Holland, on the 9th November. A provisional government was formed under social democrat Friedrich Ebert, and Germany became a republic. Events were now moving very fast and the war was racing towards its conclusion.

The War is Won, Victory is Ours, screamed the headline of that great British Institution, the News of the World newspaper, on Sunday November 10th 1918. Other news items on the front page included, *Yanks advance - France freed- Allies enter the Dardanelles- Austrian Armistice- British close to Mons- Guards enter the great fortress of Maubeuge - Surrender certain.*

The newspaper even printed an unofficial forecast list of the demands it thought that the victors should make on the soon to be defeated Germans.

Although at face value this was hardly good news for the incarcerated German service personnel held in this country, it did signify that the end of the war was imminent, and raised the prospect of release and a return home for the prisoners.

The armistice was signed in a railway carriage in the Forest of Compiegne, when a Franco-British delegation headed by Marshal Foch offered terms to the hard pressed Germans, who had no other option but to accept.

Some of the Allies large field guns continued to pound away remorselessly, firing heavy explosive shells at the enemy lines, right up until the 11 o'clock deadline on the morning of 11th November 1918, the specifically stated time of the ceasefire. Then, and only then, did all the guns fall silent and the hostilities cease. Although negotiation was still going on regarding the fine details of the agreement, and the actual peace treaty wasn't signed officially until June the following year, for all intents and purposes, the war had ended. The Great War, also called the war to end all wars, had finally come to an end. It had taken a terrible toll on the participants in a lot of ways. In the loss of life alone it had cost an estimated 10 million lives on both sides, and double that amount were wounded. Great celebrations were held all over Europe, whose populations were relieved to be free of the conflict, and just wanted to return to a normal existence as soon as possible.

At this time of worldwide rejoicing towards the end of 1918, the German prisoners in Harperley working camp had everything to look forward to; the long awaited end of the war had arrived. The prisoners were anticipating their repatriation, and reunion with their loved ones.

November and December is generally a pleasant time of year, with Christmas fast approaching. The months have a charm of their own, despite the short dark days and cold weather. Especially so with the prospect of seeing loved ones and family again after a long absence. Even more so with four years of hostilities between nations having just come to an end.

Imagine that you are a German prisoner of war incarcerated in a camp in the north of England in November 1918. The armistice has recently been signed, signalling the end to hostilities, and now there is nothing at all to prevent you going home.

Ironically and very sadly, it was at just this particular time that 27 of the prisoners died within a few weeks of each other, between the 7th of November 1918 and the 23rd November 1918.

The records at Durham Record Office hold the burial details of St James' Church in Hamsterley village, and the others for the surrounding areas. I had visited the record office and routinely searched through the local newspaper files, church registers, and other records of the period, in an half-hearted way, without much conviction, trying to find a mention however brief regarding the camp, or the prisoners.

I actually did find, not just a mention, but something spectacular, the burial records of not one or two, but 27 German prisoners of war. Perhaps there was a mass escape attempt, was my initial thought, and maybe these men were killed attempting to get away? On closer inspection I discovered that they had died over a period of about three weeks, so that made the mass escape theory unlikely. I found that the entries showed that the PoWs, all of whom were German Army personnel, had been buried in the churchyard of St James' Hamsterley during those last three weeks of November 1918. The records disclosed that all these deceased German soldiers were from the camp at Harperley, but didn't give the cause of their deaths. I would have to do a little more research before the mystery was solved.

The first Swiss Red Cross report.

The inspection visits of the Camp at Harperley were conducted by the Swiss Legation who, being neutral in the conflict, were assigned the role of the Protecting Power for the German prisoners held here in Britain by the International Committee of The Red Cross. The Swiss Legation first inspected the camp on 18th June 1917, the inspectors being Dr F Schwyzer and Dr A. L. Vischer. I have copied their report here in full with the kind permission of the Swiss Federal Archives.

The report is typed on notepaper headed

SWISS LEGATION
German Division
9 Carlton House terrace
London S. W. 1.

and is addressed to

His Excellency
Monsieur Gaston Carlin
Swiss Minister
London

Sir,
We have the honour to submit a report covering a visit of inspection to the prisoners of War Working camp at HARPERLEY, on June 18th 1917.

This camp was opened on September 16th 1916, and is dependent upon Leigh. It is about 1 mile distant from Harperley station.

DIRECTION.
The Commandant is Major A. Rouse and Dr. Garbutt of Wolsingham, the medical officer-in-charge.

PRISONERS.
There are 230 German Military prisoners at work here; the senior is Fedwebel (Sergeant) Knieschke.

DESCRIPTION OF CAMP.
The area of the camp is 100 by 90 yards, and includes 10 buildings, 8 of which are dormitories, each measuring 60 feet by 18 feet and having accommodation for 28 men.

They have wooden floors; asbestos lined walls and roofs covered with tarred felt.

Each man has a paliasse and four blankets.

The huts are heated by stoves and lighted by three hanging lamps.

The dining hall, which serves also as a recreation hall, accommodates 180 men.

There are three cells, which were unoccupied on the day of our visit.

SANITARY ARRANGEMENTS.
A reservoir connected with a small brook supplies the camp with sufficient water for ordinary purposes. The drinking water, which is excellent, comes from a neighbouring

spring.

The latrines (pail system), the twelve shower baths, with hot and cold water, and the ablution hut, are good. A drying room is provided.

The sewerage is drained into a septic tank with a filter bed, and the garbage is incinerated.

NUTRITION.

The kitchen contains two roasting ovens, and has adjacent meat and provision stores, the bread is supplied by the Army Service Corps. All the prisoners at this camp receive the additional ration for workers.

The canteen is run by the Army Canteen Committee. A 5% rebate of the profits is used by the Commandant for such improvements as the prisoner's desire.

MEDICAL INFORMATION.

The infirmary hut has two hospital beds. Two Royal Army Medical Corps orderlies are attached.

Dr. Garbutt visits the camp twice a week, or more often if necessary. No serious illness has occurred, the average of illness being 2%. Serious cases would be sent to Newcastle.

One of the prisoners of war, a professional dentist, does good work in the camp.

WORK.

The prisoners are employed by the government in ganister stone quarrying. Foremen are paid 2d (one pence), an hour skilled labourers 1 and1/2d and unskilled labourers 1d an hour, working for 48 hours a week. The camp workers are paid as follows: -

Tailor	1 and 1/2d an hour.
Shoemaker	1 and 1/2d an hour.
Clerk	3/4d an hour.
Cook	1d an hour.

Fatigue workers are detailed in turn and do not receive pay.

RECREATION.
A recreation field adjoins the camp. Many vegetables and flower gardens have been laid out.

There is a library of 150 volumes. The prisoners do some woodcarving. They have also organised a string orchestra.

Mail.
Letters and parcels from Germany take 7-8 weeks in transit.

DIVINE SERVICE.
Religious services are held on Sundays and on special festivals.

RESUME.
No complaints were made about the camp, but we received some requests for more food, better mail service and more pay. The mental condition of the prisoners in this camp is good; they all appreciate the Commandant and respect Feldwebel Kneschke, who shows much tact in dealing with the men.

The Special Attache's signatures were at the end of the report.

The International Red Cross

The Red Cross had representatives in all European countries, and was active during times of hostilities, guaranteeing that the rights of prisoners of war were respected.

Prisoner of war camp visits were undertaken by representatives of the International Committee of the Red Cross, and covered topics such as accommodation, food, clothing, health and well being of the prisoners. Copies of the reports were sent to the relevant governments, the detaining power who held the prisoners, and to the government of the prisoners' origin.

The Red Cross and Red Crescent had national organisations in some 38 different countries. The International Committee of the Red Cross was set up to coordinate the work done between these individual organisations, and to collate and direct recourses and operations. Its first conference was held in Geneva in 1863, and its duties were somewhat long-windedly defined by the Karlsruhe International Conference in 1887. 'Its purpose was to maintain and develop relations between central Committees, to serve as a central body and intermediary between them, to uphold the fundamental and uniform principles underlying the institution of the Red Cross, in short to deal with everything concerning international relations between Red Cross Societies working to relieve the wounded and sick and, in wartime to set up international agencies to assist prisoners of war'.

During July and August 1914 a number of countries joined in the war, Austria-Hungary, Russia, Montenegro, Germany, France, Belgium, Luxembourg and Great Britain. Soon the ICRC was inundated with requests for medical supplies, and medical staff. Doctors and nurses from various national Red Cross agencies from neutral countries were sent to assist, and a central agency was set up to look after the interests and well-being of the increasing numbers of prisoners of war.

The Red Crosses internationally recognised humanitarian concerns included rules agreed at the Geneva Convention 6 July 1906, and the Hague Convention 18 October 1907. These included the protection of the wounded and sick. That the neutrality of medical establishments and the medical and religious personnel of land forces be respected. The protection of hospital ships, the shipwrecked, the wounded and sick in the war at sea. The protection of prisoners of war, and the regulations respecting the Laws and Customs of War on Land, The protection of civilians and neutral persons, and regulations concerning the interment of belligerent troops in neutral territory.

Prisoners of war were guaranteed some protection under the various Conventions, but there was, as yet, no standard international rules regarding their conditions. This was not finally achieved until 1929.

The Red Cross set up the International Prisoner of War Agency on the 21 August 1914, and soon enquiries were flowing into its headquarters in Geneva at the rate of between two and three thousand letters a day. The majority of the letters sought information regarding news of a friend or relative missing at the front, evacuated, or cut off in enemy territory. The ICRC would pass these requests on to the relevant national Red Cross organisation, which could investigate the case, and find an answer to the enquiry. Information flowed both ways through the PoW agency, to and from the national investigation agencies and the enquirers.

The ICRC very soon took this a stage further and got agreements from the belligerent powers, that they would send lists of all prisoners they had captured to the enemy authorities. This was done via diplomatic channels, with copies going to the ICRC, who could then pass on information directly to any enquirer. These, and other such agreements between the warring nations, depended entirely on good will and reciprocity. Great Britain agreed to this measure on 6 October 1914.

The system helped, but was by no means perfect. As more and more countries entered the war, the task of collating the prisoners became much greater. The agency tried a new tactic. They sent forms to every prisoner requesting information about comrades in their own units. The forms asked such questions as, 'Have the persons listed below been wounded, captured or killed?' and asked that the forms be passed amongst the other prisoners. In this manner the French prisoners of war alone accounted for 90,000 missing persons not included in the official lists.

At the end of the war another 400,000 Germans fell into the hands of the Allies, and were made prisoners, adding to the numerous humanitarian and administrative problems.

The second Swiss Red Cross report.

The second inspection report is dated some eight months after the first, and produced more information.

Again addressed to His Excellency the Swiss minister Monsieur Gaston Carlin in London, it was as follows-

Monsieur le Ministre,

I have the honour to submit a report covering a visit of inspection to the working camp for combatant prisoners of war at <u>HARPERLEY</u>, Durham, on February 28th 1918.

This camp is now dependent upon Catterick

PREVIOUS VISITS.

Harperley camp has been previously visited by Dr. F. Schwyzer and Dr. A. L. Vischer, of the staff of this Legation, on June 18th 1917, and a report was addressed to you under date of September 7th 1917.

DIRECTION.

Major A. Rouse is still in command. Dr. Menzies, from Wolsingham, is now camp physician, and Lieut. Watts, interpreter.

PRISONERS.

There are, in all, 230 German prisoners at this camp, including 1 Feldwebel, 8 non-commissioned officers and 1 sailor. Vizefeldwebel Wilhelm Boog (92. Inf. Reg.) has acted as camp leader since December 13th 1917.

DESCRIPTION OF CAMP.

The camp is pleasantly situated in open country. The housing, sanitary arrangements and nutrition have been fully described in the previous report of September 7th 1917. No changes of importance, with the exception of the new food restrictions imposed by the War Office, have taken place since that date. The drinking water comes from a neighbouring spring and every facility is given for boiling water procured from any other source.

MEDICAL INFORMATION.

The general health of the prisoners is good. At the time of my visit only two patients, both suffering from slight ailments, were in the infirmary. Additional accommodation is provided in the adjoining British camp hospital, to which prisoners of war could, if necessary, be transferred.

WORK.

The work performed and wages received are the same as specified in the previous report. About half the number of men are employed at piecework, earning up to 2/- (ten pence) a day. Saturday afternoons are free.

PRISONERS LIFE.

Recreation.

Opportunities for recreation are offered, as described in the previous report.

Divine Service.

Divine Service is held almost every Sunday.

Mail

The prisoners stated that there is some delay in the arrival of letters and parcels from Germany.

RESUME.

I received no complaints form the prisoners at this camp. The installations are good and the management efficient. The men seem well behaved and, as far as it is possible under the circumstances, contented with their life and surroundings.

I have the honour to be
Monsieur le Ministre
Your most obedient humble servant
A. de Stusler
Special Attache.

This second visit was only eight or nine months or so before the fatalities, and on both visits everything seemed to be all right in the camp, so what could have been the cause of the deaths, was it a mass escape attempt? Surely not this late in 1918, just as the war was coming to an end, with the prospect of repatriation just around the corner?

Although both of the Red Cross reports maintained that the mental condition of the men was good, it is hard for us to understand precisely what thoughts and emotions these men had experienced. A lot of the prisoners must have been involved in the fiercest of battles, fighting in the trenches of the Western Front, at places like the Somme, Mons and Ypers, and it is hard for us to envisage the terrible experiences some of them must have been through. Some must have had physical wounds, and a lot more would be mentally scarred by the terrible things they had experienced during the conflict.

During the war there were accusations from both sides of atrocities committed by the other. In the heat of battle or in its immediate aftermath, it isn't easy to change from a man fighting for his very existence, amongst the blood and flesh of his dead and dying comrades, to being a civilised human being again.

Locked up in a camp, far from their Fatherland, out in the wilds of the difficult to access, English countryside. Trudging tiredly to and from the quarry high on the Fell every day. Cooped up in the cold confinement of the camp, with hundreds of other men, surviving with few comforts or luxuries, and being separated indefinitely from their friends and families. Not knowing what is happening to relations and loved ones back home must have been a terrible ordeal for these men. Even more so when their country was involved in such a savage struggle for survival.

My next stop was the record office at Bishop Auckland. There I eventually managed to obtain a copy of one of the deceased prisoner's death certificates.

There hadn't been a mass escape attempt from the camp. Nothing so melodramatic had accounted for the prisoner's deaths. The certificate solved the mystery. It stated the cause of death to be Influenza. I later discovered that all the others were the same. They had all died of 'flu.

The Influenza Epidemic of 1918.

The 'flu epidemic of 1918 was a deadly one. Originally called the Spanish Influenza Epidemic, it was the severest 'flu outbreak of the twentieth century. The disease normally takes its greatest toll on the weak, the very old and the very young, but this outbreak killed the fit and strong as well.

Its name is derived from the word influence, as it was at first thought to be present in the air all around us. We now know that Influenza is spread by a virus passed from person to person by close contact, and coughs and sneezes. Once in the lungs the virus multiplies and spreads, infecting the lung tissue, causing inflammation and a build up of mucus. Aching joints and muscles, a splitting headache, and a high temperature occur within two days, but the infection remains in the system for five days, generally producing diarrhoea, vomiting, fatigue, and a sore throat. Pneumonia can often result. Victims had a one in 15 chance of dying from the virus during the 1918 outbreak.

Influenza epidemics occur regularly, almost every year, and bad viruses appear about every two or three years. It is constantly mutating. It is thought that new strains generally originate in animals in Asia, where people live in close proximity with animals, and the risk of a virus crossing the species barrier is greater.

The 1918-19 virus was a particularly virulent strain, and although the exact cause of the outbreak is not known, it is thought to have originated in pigs. It caused the deaths of an estimated 30-50 million people worldwide.

The first recorded outbreak started in Kansas in America sometime in 1917, and quickly spread across the nation, effecting a quarter of the population. In Philadelphia the disease killed 7 people in the first week it arrived, 2,600 the second week, and 4,500 the third. In some towns and cities the rapid number of deaths overwhelmed the communities, causing chaos, as police, firemen, and even gravediggers succumbed to the infection. Children starved locked in houses alongside their dead parents. Coffins piled up in the streets awaiting burial, and relatives often had no other choice but to dig graves, and bury their deceased loved ones themselves.

The disease was taken to Europe by US soldiers who were going to the front to fight against the Germans. The troopships were ideal breeding ground for the disease, and it killed some 4,000 soldiers on the ships before they even arrived in France, and then spread rapidly though the troops in the trenches at the front line.   There   was some suspicion at first amongst the Allies that the Germans might have deliberately caused the outbreak, but this was obviously untrue as they also lost a quarter of a million lives to the virus. Others put forward the theory that the decaying corpses in no-man's land at the front, blown up by exploding shells, and mixing with poisoned gas, had somehow caused the infection.

The virus attacked in three separate waves, and soon it had swept the world, intensifying its potency as it spread. By the following year it had become the biggest single killer since the Black Death. 700,000 people were killed in America. 12,500,000 died in India, and 230,000 in Britain. The virus spread rapidly, and had an absolutely devastating effect on the population of the whole world. A population who had virtually no resistance or immunity to this strain of the disease at all.

The epidemic had a profound effect on all aspects of life in Britain. It didn't discriminate between rich or poor, and had as much effect on the upper classes as on the lower. The headmaster of Harrow, one of the countries leading public schools, acting on medical advice, sent letters to the parents of pupils in November 1918, warning them to keep their children at home while the epidemic ravaged. A total of 400 influenza cases were treated at the school, and the school staff was hard put to cope with the work. The headmaster remarked on the toll the extra work had taken on his staff and the servants. (The use of the word servants is a reminder of the sharp social differences, and attitudes in our society not so very long ago). The local District Medical Officer of Health directed the disinfection operations in the school. Only those boys due to be conscripted and required to attend army medical examinations were advised to return.

Thousands were killed by the disease in the north east of England. There were hundreds of deaths every week in the densely populated areas of Newcastle and Sunderland. Durham and some of the surrounding areas were just as badly hit, if not worse. Newspaper reports of the time said that influenza was ravaging the country.

Health committees blamed the rapid spread on the wartime conditions, stress, and the lack of proper nourishing food. Newspaper advertisements offered protection from the 'flu from medicines such as Dr Hunter's Fever Cure, which sold at one shilling and one pence a bottle, (about five pence) and claimed to be 'a recognised prophylactic in cases of influenza', and promised to ward off possible attacks.

Durham County Council later blamed the high death toll on the lack of pre-arranged, co-ordinated efforts, and with hindsight recommended a number of preventative measures in the event of further epidemics. These included a number of measures to be taken by the District Sanitary Authorities including, increasing the numbers of nurses, and having adequate reserves in case of emergencies such as Influenza, Measles, epidemics of diarrhoea and the like, and promised grants towards the costs of providing midwives and maternity nurses. Health visitors were short on the ground, there being only 60 to cater for a population of almost one million. They were recommended to act as organisers rather than to perform nursing duties, thereby being able to help a lot more than one or two patients, and in this way aid the relief work.

The setting up and maintaining of a Home Help Service was recommended. These women would be respectable and of a suitable age, without children, and be employed in homes where the mother couldn't work because of illness. They would be paid 20/- (one pound) a week, 32/- (£1.60) if food was not provided, and would be paid more if the illness was infectious. In certain cases where the patient was an expectant or a nursing mother, the council would be prepared to meet the full cost of the Home Help.

The Council also recommended the setting up of an emergency committee, made up of members of the local health committees, the Medical Officer of Health and representatives of local doctors, nursing associations and of voluntary workers. These committee members would liase with the Sanitary Inspector, health visitors and the district nurses.

Aid posts should be set up in schoolrooms, council offices welfare centres and such places. Stores of nursing requirements such as bedpans, Macintoshes, feeding cups, pneumonia jackets and supplies of dried milk and Bovril should be stockpiled at such centres. It was also recommended that isolation wards be arranged in hospitals to cater only for epidemic cases.

Dr. Modlin, acting chairman of the Sunderland Health Committee stated that over half the fatalities were from tenement style buildings where there were three or more families were living. The Sunderland and South Shields epidemic was raging with much severalty. Local doctors held meetings to discuss the outbreak, and gave advice to the public. Fresh air was reported to be the best way to avoid the disease, and people were advised to avoid crowds. Schools were closed forthwith, and the teachers advised to take their pupils' outdoors to the coast or the countryside, and hold lessons there, in the open air, instead. Worst hit were the people living in the overcrowded conditions of the slum areas.

The local newspapers reported 354 deaths from 'flu in Durham for the week ending 2nd December 1918, and 106 deaths were reported in Newcastle, where the epidemic seemed to be abating somewhat. The Registrar General's figures reported the total deaths for the country for the week to be 5,319 in the large 96 towns of England. The effect of the epidemic was so bad that undertakers complained that they were being overwhelmed as they struggled to cope with the large demand for coffins, and temporary mortuaries were used to store the bodies. On the 5th December 1918 the Stanley News reported 63 deaths from 'flu in Chester-le-Street. At Spennymore things were so bad that corpses were taken directly to the cemetery for burial, bypassing the usual funeral rituals.

The epidemic carried on remorselessly until the end of the year, and then through into the New Year. Eventually it gradually lessened in intensity in the area, and passed on to other, hapless victims in other parts of the country.

Almost certainly the cramped living conditions of the camp contributed to the severity of the outbreak amongst the prisoners. The local population only had a few deaths, which were due to the epidemic in the same period. Ironically, the highest number of prisoners died on 11th November, the very day the armistice was signed.

The bodies were interred in the churchyard of St James' at Hamsterley. The vicar presiding over the funerals. It was around this time that the British government announced the 20,000 German prisoners of war were to be repatriated, and that 14,000 had already been sent home. But this didn't help the deceased prisoners at Harperley.

St James' Church Hamsterley.

St James' Church Hamsterley dates from the 12 century, and has had some 30 incumbents during its existence. It is curiously situated a third of a mile from the actual village of Hamsterley, and no one seems to know the reason why. The church was originally built as a Chapel of Ease for St Andrew's Auckland. St James' church records date from the 1580,s and contain details of the births, deaths and marriages of the villagers, as well as the landed gentry. There are a number of very old gravestones in the churchyard, including one that has curious Celtic-like whorl markings, and a human figure carved on it. A sundial above the Norman style south porch is dated 1803 and bears the inscription *'Man fleeth as a shadow'*, a pertinent reminder of our human transience.

It must have been a really poignant funeral scene, and one that was repeated often over those three weeks in the grey month of November 1918. The church graveyard very cold and probably frost covered in the shadow of the old church. The harsh grimness of the grey old gravestones softened a little by the white covering, the holly guarding the porch providing the only splash of colour in the grey morning light. The sounds muffled as the graves were dug by the working party from the camp. A sad, silent procession making its ghostlike way from the horse-drawn cart at the entrance to the churchyard, to the church door, and entering the ancient building through the porch. Then, after the service, carrying the coffins to the waiting graves. The same working party standing to attention under the stark old sycamore trees as the coffins were lowered into the ground,

70

acting as an impromptu honour guard for their comrades.

The magnificent views across the Wear valley away to the east hidden, shrouded in dense freezing fog. The black gowned priest, shivering in the cold, grasping his bible close to him as he read the words from the Twenty Third Psalm over the open graves. His words needing no translation for the benefit of nearby German prisoners. The only other witnesses a couple of elderly villagers who looked on curiously, but respectfully, from a distance.

The party's footsteps magnified as they crunched through the cold crispness of the silent churchyard, passing the church and returned to the gate after the formalities were complete. The only other sound the stark cries of the large black crows as they soared above the tall barren trees. The white breath of the waiting horses hanging hazily in the air as the animals moved their feet on the frozen ground, cold and impatient to be moving. The men's thoughts still with the deceased men as they boarded the transport for the uncomfortable return journey to the camp.

The Victims.

The deceased men's names, arranged in alphabetical order, and dates of death are as follows-

BALZKE Alfred Paul Alwin.	13 11 1918
BECK Karl Edmund	17 11 1918
BEDORF Anton	16 11 1918
BERTHOLDT Fritz	11 11 1918
BLANKEFORT Franz Bernard	14 11 1918
BRAUNIGEN Kurt	17 11 1918
FINK Karl Edward Wilhelm	12 11 1918
FISCHER Otto	12 11 1918
GARLING Ernst Klaus Friedrich	11 11 1918
GRASSOFF Arthur	15 11 1918
HADLA Edward	11 11 1918
HORWEGE Willy Klaus. August	15 11 1918
KAUSSMANN Hensonn Gustav	17 11 1918
KEMPE Ernst	14 11 1918
KRINN Heinrich Max	18 11 1918
LANGE Alfred Karl John	11 11 1918
LEHMANN Richard.	12 11 1918
MEIER Rudolf Max Heinrich.	23 11 1918
MERKLE Ernst Heins	13 11 1918
ROSNICK Otto Karl	11 11 1918
RUDLOFF Alfred Paul	13 11 1918
SCHINK Albert	8 11 1918
SCHNEIDER Kurt Gustav	15 11 1918
SCHWENDLER Willy	12 11 1918
STERNBERG Paul Ernst Friedrich	7 11 1918
WALKOWIAK Anton	17 11 1918
WLOCZYK Felix	8 11 1918

The first death was on Thursday the 7th November 1918, and the last on Saturday the 23rd November. The most deaths, five, occurred on Monday the 11th, followed by four on Tuesday the 12th. The fatalities then tapered off with three deaths on Wednesday the 13th, and two on the 14th, before increasing again with three on the 15th, and another four on the 17th. There was only one death on Monday the 18th, and then no more until the final casualty on Saturday the 23rd. The epidemic had accounted for the lives of 27 of the prisoners, almost 12% of the camp's inmates.

The ranks of the deceased were variously described-
Six were listed as Musketiers (riflemen).
Two were described as Schützer (marksmen or sharpshooters, perhaps trained snipers).
Three were Füsiliers (riflemen).
Five were recorded as being reservists.
Three are listed as Gefreiters (lance corporals).
One Hussar, (a cavalryman).
One Offizier stellvertreter (an acting officer).
One Jäger, (a sort of mountain soldier, who sometimes operated on skis).
One was a Germeiner (a common soldier).
Two were recorded as Wehrmann (which is an old Swiss term for soldiers).
One Kriegsfreiwilliger (which means a volunteer).
One Tambour (a drummer).
All the deceased were German Army personnel.

Recorded as being present at each of the deaths was either G. Williams, or A. Buckle, presumably the two British Medical Attendants from the Royal Army Medical Corps mentioned in the inspection report, and who doubtless were involved in treating the sick men.

Six of the men were of the Roman Catholic faith.
A. Bedorf,
F.B. Blankefort.
E. Hadla.
A. Schink.
A. Walkowiak
F. Wloczyk.

They were buried in the graveyard of St James' at Hamsterley, the same as their comrades, but the R.C. priest from the Wolsingham parish of St Thomas of Canterbury officiated at their funerals, not the Vicar at St James'.

The two prisoners who died on the 8th November, Schink and Wloczyk, were buried in a different part of the churchyard from the others for some reason, perhaps because of lack of space, their position being described as 'south side new ground'.

The surviving prisoners contributed towards the cost of a memorial for their deceased comrades. This was erected in the churchyard. It was probably removed when the bodies were moved as no sign of it now remains

There was no further deaths or burials at all at St James' until the following March, so it appears that the local civilian population had escaped the worst of the epidemic.

The 200 or so remaining prisoners were repatriated to Germany, returning to their homes, joining the millions of others making their way back from the conflict. The camp, the home to a lot of the prisoners for two years, was now deserted, soon became derelict, and was demolished.

Exhumation.

The bodies of the 27 men lay there, all but forgotten, until exactly 43 years later, when on the 15th November 1961, the Consistory Court Of The Diocese Of Durham facilitated the disinterment of the bodies. Then in 1962, a Home Office licence for the removal of human remains was issued under section 25 of the Burial Act 1857, for removal of the remains of members of the German Armed Forces.

The following details, and those recorded above regarding the deceased prisoners, are reproduced with the kind permission of the parish of St James Hamsterley, and the Durham County Record Office.

Conditions of the Licence were that-

(1) Each removal shall be effected with due care and attention to decency, early in the morning: if each removal cannot be effected early in the morning, the ground in which the remains are interred shall be screened from the public gaze while the work is in progress.

2) Freshly made ground lime shall be freely sprinkled over the coffins, the soil, and if it should be necessary, elsewhere.

(3) As soon as the identity of the remains it is required to identify has been established, the coffins containing the remains shall be placed in the approved plastic containers.

(4) The removals shall be carried out under the supervision and to the satisfaction of the Medical Officer of Health for

the district.

(5) The remains shall be forthwith conveyed safely and decently to the German Military Burial Ground, Cannock Chase, Staffordshire, and there be re-interred, or if transportation cannot be immediately carried out, they shall be deposited in a Mortuary and kept safely and decently until transportation and re-interment can be effected.

The Licence states that it merely exempts from the penalties, which would be incurred if the removal took place without a licence: it does not in any way alter civil rights. It does not, therefore, confer the right to bury the remains in any place where such right does not already exist. The Licence is signed at the Home Office in Whitehall be Secretary of State R. A. Butler, and dated the 3rd of May 1963.

The Home Office wrote to the Vicar of St James' Hamsterley on the same day, and informed him that the work would take place.

The bodies were duly disinterred and taken to the German War Grave Cemetery at Cannock near Birmingham, as part of an agreement made on 16th October 1959 between the government of the United Kingdom and Northern Ireland and the Federal Republic of Germany, that the Volksbund Deutsche Kriegsgraberfursorge (The German war Graves Commission) to take over the concentration of the graves of German war dead buried in Great Britain and Northern Ireland on behalf of the German Federal Government.

The Volksbund provides assistance to the next of kin in tracing the location of graves, arranges for wreaths to be laid on the graves, and for photographs to be taken of them if requested by relatives. It organises, and conducts tours of the cemeteries, and strives continuously to draw the attention of the younger generation to the events of the two world wars and the subsequent disastrous results.   A central war cemetery for the German dead at Cannock Chase grouped most of the German war dead together in one place. This is an obvious advantage for the care of the graves, and for the convenience of relatives seeking the final resting place of their loved ones. As many as 6000 dead of both world wars were buried in more than 700 different sites in civil cemeteries and church graveyards in Britain.

As no fighting took place on British soil at all during the First or Second World Wars, most of the German casualties died in prisoner of war or internment camps, or consisted of air crews shot down over Britain, or washed ashore on the coast. The first reburials took place in the United Kingdom in 1962 and 1963, the bodies from Hamsterley being amongst the first to be moved. Later reburials followed in 1966 and 1967.

Most of the local authorities readily gave their permission for the bodies to be relocated, but a few refused, and insisted that the graves remain where they were for specific reasons. Some of the graves could not be reopened because the dead lay buried in communal graves with British civilian dead. In some instances the deceased's relatives also refused to give their permission to remove their loved ones from where they were buried, preferring them to remain at peace in their original position.

Those that couldn't be moved still have their graves cared for by the Commonwealth War Graves Commission, or are cared for by Local Authorities on the Commissions behalf.

Those war dead still in municipal cemeteries have markers that are easily identifiable because of the special apical shape of the headstones.

The recent discovery of a 1,000lb unexploded German bomb in Sunderland, (and the subsequent disruption this caused in the east end of the city), brought back memories of an air raid in September 1940, when a German bomber was shot down, and the four crew killed. They were buried with full military honours in Castletown cemetery, where they still remain today. These are among a total of 1,679 war dead buried in their original graves in the United Kingdom, including some on three of the Channel Islands. Most of the German war dead however have been relocated. The proceedings being overseen by the Medical Officer of Health for the areas concerned, and conducted with great respect and solemnity according to the strict rules laid down by both governments.

These, until now, forgotten tragic events of 84 years ago at Harperley, illustrate just how vulnerable we humans are, not just to the fortunes of war, but to the forces of nature. It is a reminder of the forgotten 27 men who never returned to their homes after being captured. The men had lived for years as captives in a foreign land, and were destined never to regain their freedom again. It is a local reminder of that distant war, and of the real men with real lives, who fought in it. Men who had hopes and aspirations just like us, and who were part of a worldwide conflict that will soon perhaps just be worth a passing mention, alongside the many others, in the history books

Bibliography.

History of the International Committee of the Red Cross: from Sarajevo to Hiroshima- Henry Dunant Institute 1984.

Keep The Home Fires Burning-Propaganda in the First World War-Cate Haste, Allen Lane 1977.

The Imperial war Museum Book of the Western Front- Malcolm Brown.

The Imperial War Museum Book of the Somme- Malcolm Brown.

The Weardale Gazette.

From Pomerania to Ponteland, The Youngest Prisoner of War- Rudi Lux.

The News of the World 1918.

The Stanley News 1918.

The Sunderland Echo 1918.